Forever Family
Our Amazing Adoption Journey

Emily J. Moore

ISBN 978 0 9926935 0 3

For our precious little angels, who
we will treasure forever xx

Forever Family

Our Amazing Adoption Journey

Contents

Introduction

Over recent years we have been on an Amazing Journey, full of emotion and joy. A journey that has enabled us to become Mummy and Daddy to our two amazingly beautiful and special baby girls-our gorgeous daughters!

For the majority of people wanting children, it's a case of trying for a baby. This may take weeks, months or even years but usually happens eventually for couples. For other people like ourselves this is never an option and we take a different and even more special journey to become parents.

Throughout our adoption journey we found information about adoption, the adoption process and we were given good advice from our adoption social worker, however nothing that explained the in-depth detail of the adoption process through the eyes of people who had been there every step of the way.

I therefore felt compelled to write this book to give people an insight into what adoption was really like for us and the process we went through to enable us to become Mummy and Daddy.

I hope that this will help to give a better understanding to people who are thinking about adoption or are ready to embark on their own adoption journey and also increase people's awareness of what adoption is and what the process involves.

It is also a personal tribute to our girls, who love to hear all about when we were preparing to be their Mummy and Daddy, the time that we first saw them and how happy we felt. They also love to learn all about when they came home forever. This book will therefore be a recollection of every in-depth detail for them to read, remember and reminisce about in the future; to remind them of just how special and truly loved they really are.

Our Life Prior To Adoption

My husband and I got married quite young, I was 20 and he was 23 and having a family was something that we had always both wanted more than anything. We worked hard and saved hard ready to provide for our little ones, moving to a bigger house ready for when this day came.

Having children was always something that we assumed would just happen; when you are young you don't foresee health problems that would mean getting pregnant would just never be possible.

It wasn't until I was 28 years old, after years of trying to get pregnant that I was diagnosed with endometrial cancer and subsequently needed to undergo a hysterectomy the evening before my 29th birthday.

From this day onwards, and even before if I am honest, we knew that I would never be able to become pregnant. We had already discussed at length about adoption and we knew that we definitely wanted to adopt children, even before it was confirmed that I would never conceive.

We also believe in fate, that everything happens for a reason and we accepted that this is what was obviously planned for us. I didn't feel angry about my medical diagnosis, or dwell on it, but took comfort in that adoption was meant for us. I felt a sense of relief once the hysterectomy had been done so that we could concentrate on becoming a forever Mummy and Daddy to our children. All we ever dreamt about was having children, so we were so excited and couldn't wait to become parents to our children, who we believed were waiting for us- and they were.

Beginning Our Adoption Journey

Our Adoption Journey began in July 2009. It was shortly after my surgery but we were so eager to adopt that we decided to make the initial phone call to our local Social Services Adoption Department.

Obviously, never having been through this before, we were new to this and not quite sure what to do or who to ring, so I did an internet search about adoption in our local authority. This brought up a telephone number of the department that we needed to contact.

I remember vividly making that first phone call and speaking to an adoption social worker who asked me some questions about why we wanted to adopt. She also explained the basic adoption process to us and informed us that there was a lengthy wait; about a year before a social worker would even be able to come out to do an initial visit to discuss adoption with us and decide whether we would be suitable people to begin the adoption process.

We were a bit deflated about the long wait to even have an initial visit but accepted it and decided that we would use this time to improve our house and decorate etc, ready for when we would become parents. The social worker that I had the telephone conversation with said that she would send us a form in the post that we needed to complete about ourselves and the reasons for us wanting to adopt. We promptly completed this form and returned it and were pleased that we were now on the waiting list to begin the adoption process, even if this meant a lengthy wait.

A Very Exciting Phone Call

We had just walked through the front door following the funeral of a very special Great Aunt, the Aunt who had offered to pay for IVF before we knew that this wasn't an option. The telephone began to ring. Still teary eyed, I answered it and to our amazement it was an Adoption Social Worker informing us that they had received our initial forms back and they were ready to assign an adoption social worker to us so we could begin the Adoption Process.

We couldn't believe it! Prepared for a year's wait and now being told, a few weeks after receiving our initial forms, they were ready to start our process. We knew our Great Aunt must have been looking down on us and, one way or another, helping us to become parents. We weren't normally lucky people so we were so surprised at this amazing news.

We were given the date that our adoption social worker would visit us for our initial visit. I put the phone down, still in shock, knowing that we were a step closer to our dream of eventually becoming a Mummy and Daddy.

Initial Home Visit

After frantically cleaning the house and getting ready to make the best impression on our allocated adoption social worker, we were nervous yet very excited about her impending arrival.

We were unsure of what to expect. Up until now my only experience of social workers was through my employment on a children's ward in a hospital when we had child protection cases that needed to be investigated and they were obviously very stern and serious individuals.

There was the knock at the door that we had been waiting for and our social worker was on the doorstep. I answered the door and we were very pleasantly surprised, our social worker was a lovely middle aged lady who instantly put us at ease; she could probably sense that we were nervous but was so very friendly and charming.

We all chatted very informally about adoption and she asked more in depth questions about the reasons why we wanted to adopt and how we felt we would be able to meet the children's needs. She explained more about the adoption process and answered all of our questions.

She told us that she would be able to begin our adoption Home Study with us in a few weeks and gave us a date for November when she would return. In the meantime she left us with the task of getting as much experience together as a couple of being with and caring for children as possible.

I was lucky as I worked with children but my husband didn't have as much experience. Also it was important that we gained joint experience of looking after and caring for children as much as possible in everyday situations.

Our social worker explained that we could do this with nieces or nephews or friends' children and that we needed to keep a diary of what we did and evaluate how each visit or outing had gone.

Gaining Experience

We took every opportunity of caring for our nephew who was 4 years old at the time. We also went on outings with friends and other family members who had children in order to gain experience of caring for children and going on outings (along with their tantrums!!) in as many settings as possible.

We took photos on each occasion and kept a diary of what we did and where and how this had gone, including anything that didn't go as well as we had envisaged and explain how we dealt with certain situations and behaviours.

Along with this we also kept any pictures or paintings the children had done or created with us to show evidence of activities we had shared with them.

This built up evidence for our portfolio so that we could prove that we had gained some very valuable child experience and this could be presented at Adoption Panel so the panel members could be confident that we had experience as a couple of looking after and caring for children in a range of settings whilst doing different activities.

It's also important to mention that the social workers don't expect everything to go well and like to know about things that were less successful and the ways in which you were able to deal with these situations. Let's face it, children can be very unpredictable and there is normally an occasion on every outing where something may go in a way which you hadn't planned!

The Assessment and Home Study

November eventually arrived and we can began our Assessment and Home Study: a very exciting time, we felt that we were now properly embarking on our Adoption Journey and getting closer to eventually having children.

I sort of compared this stage to getting pregnant and the joyous emotion that you will hopefully one day become a parent as long as everything goes well over the next few months. The time scale is also similar as the home study takes at least six months and often longer.

I know a lot of friends were shocked that it was taking so long; they thought that once we were accepted it was a matter of the social worker finding us suitable children. It can get quite tedious as the majority of people will ask you daily if there is any news of children yet, and you find yourself constantly repeating that it's not just a case of them finding suitable children, you have to go through a lengthy process first and be approved by the Adoption Panel before children are even considered for you. These people mean well but once I had explained to them on numerous occasions about the process, I ended up just saying "No not yet!"

Luckily as we were accepted to proceed with the adoption process our Assessment could now begin, so we completed the Application Forms with our social worker.

The application form required factual information about ourselves and we had to give consent for a number of checks to be undertaken about us both, this was to ensure that there weren't any reasons why we were not suitable to adopt.

We had to provide a number of references to include a family reference. We asked each of our parents to complete these as you are required to have one for each person who is adopting. They provided a written reference for us and then our social worker would follow this up with a visit to ask them more detailed questions about us.

I know that they were quite nervous about being interviewed by a social worker, not because they didn't feel that we were suitable to adopt, but because of how social workers can be perceived. They worried about being able to answer all of the questions that they were asked, as they obviously knew how much this meant to us both, and felt pressure not to let us down. We had already met our social worker and were confident that she would put them at ease as we explained to them just how friendly and 'human' she was.

I know they were pleasantly surprised by her and all of them commented on just how nice she was. They managed to answer all of the questions and said it was more like a general chat about us to find out what we were like as a couple from their perspective, and how they thought we would cope as parents.

We also needed two personal references and we both asked our good friends to provide these for us and again this was followed up with a visit to each of them by our social worker.

My friend was heavily pregnant at the time and again rather anxious about a social worker visiting, but I reassured her that our social worker was not intimidating, but really friendly and easy to talk to. After the visit my friend agreed that she was lovely and had just asked her questions about how we were as a couple and how she thought we would be as parents. The visits were quite lengthy though, over an hour in duration with each person giving the references, but if you choose somebody who knows you inside out they will have no problem talking about you for an hour!

We had to provide an employer's reference as we were both employed. These were just written references though and were not followed up with a visit.

They also asked for a reference from GPs, the school of any child you are currently parenting and any previous significant partners, but the latter two didn't apply to us.

We were open about wanting to adopt, so these were all fine for us, but it could be intrusive to people who aren't wanting to tell other people at this stage that they are beginning the adoption process, especially as their employers need to provide a reference so they will have to be informed even at this early stage.

Our Home Study

The Home Study and Assessment process is when the Adoption Social Worker begins to examine your suitability to adopt, and they needed to collect extensive and detailed information about ourselves to build up a complete profile of us.

Our social worker visited us regularly at home, on average every couple of weeks for at least two hours per visit, but usually longer, and she made written notes on each visit to help her with the preparation of the Adoption Report at the end of the Home Study.

She began by considering how our lives and backgrounds would influence our ability to care for and parent an adopted child. Our social worker asked us questions about our lives so far, from when and where we were born through to the present day and everything in between.

This included information about our childhood and our memories of this, our schools, family and any significant life events, through to when we met each other. This continued throughout our married life until the present day and the events that had led to us wanting to adopt children.

They are keen to learn about both positive and negative aspects of your life and how these were dealt with and how you coped in certain situations throughout your life.

It can appear very intrusive and you feel that your social worker knows you better than you know yourself after this! It also gives an opportunity to reminisce about your life and we found it an enjoyable part of the process.

It highlights your strengths and weaknesses to gain as much information about yourselves and your lifestyles to ensure that adoption is definitely the right decision for you.

Both myself and my husband also had separate interviews which we found quite strange at first but understand that it's to make sure that both people in the couple want to adopt as much as each other and it's not a case of one person pushing the other into adoption.

Pets will also need to be assessed. We had an English Pointer dog and our social worker came to give him a test! It was just very basic to make sure that he was friendly and wouldn't object to little fingers being put into his food bowl etc.

He was very boisterous so we did worry a bit that he might fail but as he was obedient when told to do certain things and we explained that he wouldn't have the run of the house and showed that he wouldn't be intimidating to children, he passed with flying colours. Extra big treat and a gold star for him that evening!

You need to provide details of social and support networks of the people who would be there for you once you have children and in what ways you anticipate that they would support you. This may include social or emotional support or practical and physical support.

A financial report is undertaken to see how much you earn and what your out-goings are, although it is important to mention that they don't refuse adopters on financial grounds and single and unemployed people can adopt.

They need to check that your neighbourhood and community is suitable for children, so you have to show evidence that there are child resources and facilities locally. This is a good opportunity to make some enquiries into what your local area offers for children, if you aren't already aware. Most areas have parent and toddler groups and 'Sure Starts', which are run by the local authority, and provide some good activities and groups for parents and children, including toddler groups, music and cookery time and sensory rooms etc.

They are also keen to learn about the nurseries and schools that you may consider for your children.

Copies of documents such as car insurance, house insurance, driving licences and birth and marriage certificates will need to be taken by the Social Worker, along with any exam or qualification certificates. A Criminal Records check will be also need be undertaken, which your social worker will gain your permission to carry out.

The social worker will explain in great detail about the additional needs that a lot of children waiting for adoptive parents will have, a common one being children who are affected by alcohol and drug misuse during pregnancy. They are very supportive about what you feel your abilities would be to care for a child with special needs and you are not pressurised in any way if you feel out of your depth to adopt children with specific special or additional needs.

Lots of discussions also take place about the type, age and sex of child you would like to adopt and if you would like one child or a sibling group.

We kept an open mind about gender and adopting children with additional needs, although we stated that we would like to adopt two children who were siblings. We explained that we would like children who were as young as possible, preferably under 4 years old, to allow valuable nurturing and bonding time before they began school, which we felt was important.

It appears that some people are very particular even down to eye and hair colour!

A home safety check is carried out during this process and the social worker checks to ensure your house is safe and tells you of anything you need to do to ensure it is safe. This includes having smoke alarms, window locks, stair gates and socket safety covers. They will also need to make sure you have adequate bedrooms and space for the number of children that you are wishing to adopt, giving you a timescale to make any adjustments to your house.

You keep a file with all the paperwork and information that relates to the Home Study which includes any tasks or work that you have completed which provides evidence that you are competent in each area needed to complete the Home Study and Assessment process and show that you are suitable to be adoptive parents.

Medicals are undertaken by your GP and the information is passed to the Adoption Medical Advisor. You don't get to see these but they are quite straight forward to include height and weight, blood pressure etc. but also requires the doctor to assess your medical history and consult your medical records to see is they are confident that you are suitable to adopt.

In certain circumstances additional medicals or reports are requested and in my case my gynaecology consultant needed to do a report. These can be very stressful at the time and I was so worried that I may not be able to adopt, with my recent past medical diagnosis. We would have been so devastated if these medicals had failed and we couldn't continue the process to adopt.

I think it's only natural to worry when you want something so much and don't want anything to stop your dreams of becoming parents. Thankfully the Adoption Medical Advisor was happy for us to continue the process.

When our social worker was confident that we had successfully completed the Home Study Assessment and had all the evidence to show we were competent in everything, meeting all the competency framework required, she arranged for another adoption social worker to do a 'second opinion' visit.

The 'second opinion' social worker will attend, together with your own social worker, to ensure that they are in agreement that you are suitable candidates to adopt. The 'second opinion' social worker had an in - depth chat and discussion with us, asking further questions, and then looked around the whole of our house, basically double checking that our house was safe and suitable for children. Again she was really lovely, very friendly and made us feel relaxed.

Adoption Preparation Group

During the Home Study and Assessment process, you have to attend an Adoption Preparation Group. The one that we attended was held over four full days and was run by the Adoption Team for our Local Authority. They hold these courses three times a year and your social worker will book you a place on one at the relevant time.

We attended ours in the January, two months after we started the adoption process with our social worker. Not knowing what to expect, we set off early for the 1.5 hour journey, not wanting to be late on the first day of our course. We arrived in plenty of time and were welcomed in by the Adoption Team and offered a hot drink which was very much appreciated on that freezing cold January morning.

We had a general chat with the social workers whilst we were waiting for everyone to arrive and they were really friendly and welcoming. The course began with everyone introducing themselves informally; there were only 10 people in our group (5 couples) who again were all really pleasant and easy to chat to.

I had been looking forward to meeting other people who were in the same situation as us and going through the same adoption process. I suppose it is similar to people at their antenatal classes when pregnant, giving an opportunity to discuss and share how everything is going.

Unlike expectant mothers, who usually know plenty of friends and family who have given birth and become parents, there are rarely people you know, to readily chat to about adoption. We didn't know of anybody else who had adopted or were going through the adoption process so thought the course would provide an excellent opportunity to chat to other prospective adopters.

I know that my husband was quite apprehensive though about this course, as unlike myself, he had not done any formal courses since leaving college 15 years ago and wasn't somebody who enjoys talking in groups or doing role play-everyone's dreaded hate!

We were pleasantly surprised as it was very informal; the majority of the course was listening to speakers and doing group work tasks. The course was very interesting and covered everything from the statistics of children who were in care, through to explaining the adoption process in great detail. A lot of work was done around what it means to bring a child or children into your life forever through adoption. We learnt about the law, orders and legislation relevant to children in care and throughout the adoption process.

A very emotionally difficult part of the course were the Safeguarding sessions (formerly known as Child Protection). They discussed in extensive detail about the different categories and types of abuse and the effect this abuse has on children, both at the time and throughout their lives. They explained about the work that you can do, once you have become their parents, to deal with any previous abuse that they may have suffered to best help your children to cope. Obviously a very difficult subject, especially not knowing at this point who your babies are and hoping and praying that they are not suffering this abuse, but being realistic that the majority of children waiting to be adopted have unfortunately suffered a degree of abuse-a very sad thought.

Attachment and behaviour was a big topic. Attachment is the relationship or bond that exists between an infant and the person or people who provide most of the child's care. Research has shown the importance of early relationships on the social and emotional development of children. We had a Child Psychologist who took this part of the course which was very informative.

Sadly many children who are adopted have not had their basic needs met when babies which can cause significant problems for them in the future. We learnt how essential it is to try and put back everything the child has missed out on in their early lives and we were told to imagine a brick wall with some of the bricks missing and how over time it would fall down.

The same goes for a child who has had important parts of their essential needs not met and we learnt how to try and put back these missing parts in a child's life to help them best cope. Even if this means nurturing a 4 year old like a newborn baby and doing everything for her, spoon feeding her, giving her a bottle, playing with much younger toys or rocking and singing lullabies to her. If you don't provide children with everything that they have missed out on when they were younger, then they are likely to find it very difficult to progress successfully to the next developmental stage and this can pose problems for them in the future.

Another activity that we did makes me feel emotional every time I think about it. A social worker gave us all cards with the names of different people to include birth parents, social workers, foster carers, respite foster carers, support workers, adoptive parents etc. She acted out the scene pretending to be a child in care who went (with a black bin liner with a few minimal belongings) from a birth parent, taken by a social worker to a foster carer's house, then to a respite foster carer, then to another foster carer's, back to birth parents and then to a foster carer's again etc.

This highlighted just how many placements a child in care may have had in her life before being adopted. How can she ever dare to trust that when she is adopted, she will be staying forever with her Forever Parents as she has never had this consistency in her life before, and has often been moved around so frequently to be in the care of people who are complete strangers to her?

This showed just how much these poor little children go through in the care system and how frightening it all must be for them. They are truly amazing little people who deserve so much better.

We learnt in more detail about life story work and the most effective ways to talk to children about their past, using photographs and their life story book which their own social worker will complete for them once adopted. We were told to always have their photographs accessible to them so they can get them out and you can openly discuss these together. This even applies to very young children, so even if they are too young at the time to understand that they are adopted, it is never a secret. They will start to learn about it from the earliest opportunity through their photographs and talking through it with them. Something a lot of people don't understand is that you should never have to sit them down and tell them that they are adopted when they are older; it's something that they should grow up knowing about even from babies and toddlers.

We were introduced to the Post Adoption Support Social Workers, who are there to give advice and support if ever or whenever you may need it, after you have your children placed. They are just a phone call away and are experts on adoption and the issues you may face with your children in the future.

We also had the opportunity to meet and talk to some people who had already adopted children, to discuss how it was for them and to ask them how they dealt with certain situations. They answered any questions we had and it was really useful to speak to people who had already been though the adoption process and had adopted their children, to be able to ask them how everything had gone. I think the most common question that they were asked was how long did they have to wait to be matched with their children and how well did they settle in the early days.

On the final day the Adoption Manager spoke to us about all the children that were waiting for adoptive parents in our county. This gave me butterflies! To think the children that she was discussing (obviously anonymously and not in great detail) could actually become *our* children. It filled us with hope of soon becoming Mummy and Daddy and made the experience seem so much more real when she was talking about the actual children waiting.

We really enjoyed this course and met some lovely people, some of whom we have kept in e-mail contact with. The course really made us feel more confident on the many issues that you face once you get your children and equipped us with the information to best support us and our children.

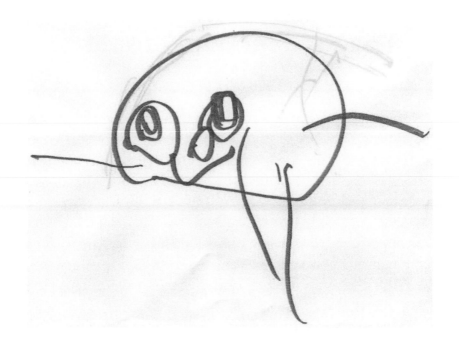

29

The Prospective Adopters Report

Once your social worker is confident that you have completed everything needed in the Home Study and Assessment process, and you are competent and ready to become adoptive parents, then the Prospective Adopters Report is written by your social worker. This is a very lengthy and detailed document, in our case 98 pages long. You then have the opportunity to read and sign this document and make any comments if needed.

Included in this report is key information about yourselves and your lives from the day you were born until the present day. It has references and copies of everything that you have completed during your Home Study; quite a surreal experience having your whole life, so far, written down in front of you, together with evidence to suggest why we were suitable adoptive parents.

This report is then given to the Adoption and Permanence Panel members about a week prior to your Adoption Panel Hearing date. This gives them the opportunity to read and learn more about you and to prepare any questions they wish to ask you at Adoption Panel.

Adoption Panel

Today is the day!! We have been working towards this day for the past 6 months. With all of our reports, The Home Study and Assessment and documentation having already been presented to the Adoption Panel members, it was our day to meet all of the people who were going to decide our fate on whether or not we would ever become parents.

Unlike the majority of people who are trying for a baby, who may be wondering *when* they would become pregnant and become parents, we knew that this decision - *if* we would ever have children - lay in the hands of these adoption panel members. The most important decision, what we had been dreaming about for all of our married lives, to have children was now going to be decided by some people that we had never met.

The Adoption Panel is accountable to our local county council through the cabinet member for Social Care and Health. It is a multi-disciplinary panel consisting of four workers from the Children and Younger Adults Department, three independent lay members, a county councillor, a Medical Advisor, a chair person, a legal advisor, an educational advisor and a professional advisor.

The panel members look at all of the information about you, your home study and assessment and reports and documentation and they then make a recommendation as to whether they consider you to be suitable adoptive parents.

Such an emotional yet nerve wracking day, a day that we had been longing for throughout our Adoption Journey, yet so anxious in case these panel members, for some reason, may not approve us and our hopes and dreams of becoming parents be shattered.

We knew that we had done everything that we possibly could and all the relevant work had been completed. We trusted that our social worker, in whom we had every faith, would not have brought us to panel if she felt in any way that we wouldn't be approved, but it didn't stop us from being nervous and worrying.

Too nervous to eat breakfast we set off early for the drive to where our Adoption Panel was being held. Preparing for every eventuality and worrying about hold ups, we set off three hours prior to our allocated panel time. The drive should have taken no more than about an hour and a half, but we preferred to be very early rather than late. We had a good journey with no delays and found the place- a large imposing Victorian Building which had a very grand appearance and we parked up. With a couple of hours to spare, we went for a walk around an adjacent park trying to pass some time. We then sat in the car park and watched as we saw all of the Panel Members arriving and entering the building of our panel hearing.

After the slowest two hours ever we decided that we would go in, ready for our Panel Hearing. We met our social worker and we were taken into a side meeting room.

Our adoption social worker and the social worker who had undertaken our second opinion visit were both present. They chatted to us about what would happen during today's panel hearing and apologised that there was a delay and they were running late. They explained that the Adoption Service Manager would come and meet us shortly and inform us of a few questions that the panel members wished to ask us and then we would be invited into the room where our Panel Hearing was taking place.

We waited nervously for a while and then the large wooden door creaked open and the Adoption Service Manager entered. She was very friendly but it didn't ease our nerves. She told us the questions that the Panel would like to ask us and then took our social worker into panel before returning a few minutes later to invite us in.

We took a deep breath, entered the room and sat down at the two empty seats waiting for us around the large board room table. All eyes were on us from the fifteen panel members and social workers, a very nerve wracking experience. Each panel member introduced him or herself and explained their role and then we were asked three straightforward questions which we answered to the best of our ability. The adoption manager then thanked us and asked us to return to the first waiting room and said that all the panel members would now vote. She would return to us to give us their decision in a few minutes.

After another nervous wait she returned and informed us that it was a unanimous YES! Every panel member had voted to approve us to be adoptive parents. I burst into tears, we were going to become Mummy and Daddy. We didn't know when, or at this stage, who our wonderful babies would be but we knew that we would one day be parents. We were so over the moon! The news that we had been wishing for had just been delivered and we were so overjoyed!

The social worker informed us that the overall decision would still lie with the Agency Decision Maker who had to agree, confirm and rubber stamp the decision but as it was a unanimous 'yes' there wouldn't be any reason for him to disagree.

The Agency Decision Maker doesn't sit on the panel or attend these hearings but has all of the information and evidence presented to him. As the overall manager, he has the final say as to whether people are approved, but he is guided by the panel's decision. If it's a unanimous 'yes' he wouldn't normally go against it, but you have to wait for his official letter as confirmation of being approved.

We left the panel still teary- eyed with joy and went out for lunch to celebrate, phoning our parents to inform them of our fantastic news. A few days later, after dashing for the post everyday just in case, the Agency Decision Maker's letter arrived in the post to confirm that he was in agreement that we should become Adoptive Parents, which was amazing!

The Wait To Be Matched

Now that we had been approved as adopters, it was the job of the Family Finder from our Local Authority Adoption Department to make potential matches of suitable children who are waiting for adoptive parents.

She looks at our reports about the sort of children that we would like to adopt and matches that with the reports of children who are waiting for adoptive parents and the requirements that they have. She considers the type of parents that would be suitable for the children and makes matches that she feels would meet both the requirements of the children and adoptive parents.

This obviously can take a considerable amount of time and we were prepared for a lengthy wait as we were told it can take many months or even years for people to have a suitable match.

I found myself doing internet searches to try and discover the average time that other adoptive parents had waited to be matched with their children. I got quite disheartened as I discovered that the majority of people had been waiting at least a year and some much longer, even up to three years!

I therefore decided that we shouldn't let ourselves get our hopes up too much. This is incredibly difficult though when all you can think about is your babies. I considered it to be like somebody being told that they were pregnant, but then saying that the length of their pregnancy was a mystery- would it be nine months or three years?!

Each day we knew that the phone could potentially ring to give us some tremendous news, and every time the phone did ring I think my heart nearly jumped out of my chest just in case it was our social worker making the call that we were dreaming about. However, being sensible, we weren't expecting it to be any time soon and had to try and carry on everyday life. It was so hard for us to think about anything else other than who our babies would be. We knew that we would one day become parents now, but had no idea when that day would come.

We felt that this was made more difficult due to the fact that you are not told about what is going on 'behind the scenes'. You have no idea about the children that the Family Finder is considering, or even if there are any children at that moment in time waiting for adoptive parents that they would consider to be a suitable match.

We tried to keep ourselves as busy as possible during the waiting period. We were told to book a holiday or do everything that we wouldn't be able to do once we have children, but, we had already had thirteen years of doing things as a couple. All we could imagine and wanted to do now was things with our children, we didn't want to book a holiday in case we missed an important call from our social worker with the news that we were waiting for: our babies!

Getting The Phone Call

It was two months after our Adoption Panel Approval and we got a phone call from our social worker who said that she would like to come and talk to us the next day! She didn't let on what the visit was about and we thought that it must be a general catch up, to stay in touch whilst we waited for a match.

Obviously we both were really hoping she was coming to deliver us the news of our lives but we didn't allow ourselves to build our hopes up.

We had a whole day at work to do first as our social worker had arranged to come at 4.30pm. There was no way that we would be able to concentrate properly at work, going over in our heads what our social worker might be coming for and day - dreaming that she might have news of children for us. At the same time though, trying to not get too excited in case she was just coming for a catch up- this was a real emotional rollercoaster!

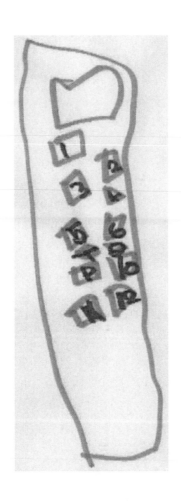

Our Social Worker Visits & Gives Us The News

Our social worker arrived, as planned, and we were obviously really pleased to see her. She sat down and gave us THE NEWS! She said that they had two little sisters waiting for a Mummy and Daddy who had been successfully matched to us. We were so overjoyed and listened excitedly as she began telling us all about them.

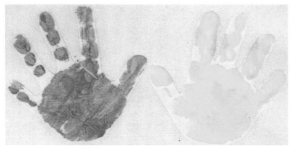

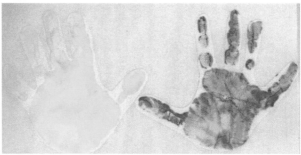

They sounded so perfect, our little girls ages 7 months and just 2 years old, and it was so emotional as she gave us lots of information about our babies. When she had finished talking, we told her how they sounded amazing and perfect for us. She said that she would give us their individual reports, which gave us information on every little detail of the girls from the day they were born, their birth, through until the present day. This included their history, why they had needed to be taken into care, about their birth parents and every detail that social services knew about their little lives so far.

An Exciting, Sleepless Night Reading

We were so excited and couldn't sleep a wink all night, we stayed awake reading their reports (all 105 pages) on each of our babies to learn every little detail about them. We read them over and over again and couldn't put their reports down. Here in front of us was information telling us all about our babies, every finest detail about them and of their little lives so far.

We fell in love with our baby daughters from that day, long before we had ever met them or even seen a photograph of them. I got up at 6am ready for work, not knowing how I could ever do a day's work. I couldn't concentrate on anything due to the excitement of the news of our babies; we just couldn't stop thinking about them and picturing them and wondering what they were doing.

Clock watching at work, I was waiting for 9 am to arrive so I could phone our social worker. I eagerly phoned her from work to tell her that we definitely wanted to become parents to these two little girls. We felt so lucky and overjoyed that we could be Mummy and Daddy to two such amazing babies.

When we told our social worker that we wanted to proceed, she said that she would arrange to come and visit us and bring the girls' social worker, so that she too could consider whether we would be suitable to adopt the girls.

They arranged this for a few days later. It was such an amazing time and I don't know how we ever contained our excitement. Trying to continue with everyday life and work, we just thought about our babies every second of every day.

Our Girls' Social Worker Visits

Eventually the day arrived when the girls' social worker would visit along with our social worker. She arrived and we all chatted together for a while and she asked us some questions and was confident that we were suitable parents for the girls.

She asked if we would like to see a photograph of our babies. What a silly question! We couldn't wait to see them! My husband and I huddled together as she passed us their pictures. They were more beautiful than words could ever express. Here in front of us were our babies. They were so cute and perfect, we couldn't believe how lucky we were to have been chosen to be their Mummy and Daddy. I burst into tears of joy and just could not stop looking at their photographs, gazing lovingly at them and longing to meet them.

Their social worker then said that she would need their photographs back as they were the only copy they had. It was so difficult to be shown a picture of your babies and then have to hand it back to the social worker. I wanted to keep them with me and feel close to them but they were now imprinted on my brain and I could close my eyes and see their little faces.

It's an image that you could never forget, seeing your babies for the first time.

They informed us that they would arrange a meeting with the girls' foster carers so that we could hear more about them on a day- to -day level and learn all their likes, dislikes, routines etc and their little personalities. I must have dreamed about our babies for the whole of the night and when I was awake and not dreaming they were forever in my thoughts.

Meeting Our Baby Girls' Foster Carers

We travelled to the Social Services building in the same town where our girls were in foster care, for the meeting with their foster carers. Knowing that we were in close proximity to our girls was a very warm feeling. We didn't know at this point the address of where they lived in foster care but knowing that we were somewhere very near to them was comforting.

I must have looked at every house that we travelled past in their town on the way to this meeting just in case we drove past their house and I could catch a glimpse of our daughters, but we didn't!

We met their foster carers who filled us in on the little details about our girls, our eldest liked 'In The Night Garden', especially Iggle Piggle. We were told what they liked to eat, their daily routines, what milk our baby was on, their nappy sizes, clothes and shoe sizes and every finest detail about them which was so lovely to hear and learn about.

At the end of the meeting the foster carers gave us a DVD which contained video clips of our girls as well as photographs. I cradled this all the way home. This was our most treasured belonging, so precious, it was photos of our babies to keep at last.

We couldn't wait to get home so that we could watch the DVD and see and feel close to our beautiful daughters. We played this constantly, watching their every move and the sounds they were making on the DVD. I was worried that we may wear this out as we just watched it constantly wishing that we were with them.

We printed out some of their photographs from this DVD and had them in frames around the house so that we could look at them all the time. It was so nice having their pictures around and we just wanted to love and hug them so much.

The wait to meet our girls was so hard. We knew every detail about them, we had some of their photographs, we had their DVD but we still were not yet able to meet our little girls.

The next step was for our social worker to write another very lengthy report document containing evidence of why we were suitable parents for our babies and how we were able to meet all of their needs. They also needed to provide evidence of how the girls were suitable for us, to ensure that we were all a good and successful match. This document was then presented to the Adoption Matching Panel a week before our matching panel date.

50

Matching Panel

Matching Panel was made up of the same people who sat on our Approval Panel but at the Matching Panel they are making recommendations as to whether they consider you to be a suitable match, to be adoptive parents for the children to whom you have been matched.

Our social worker and the children's social worker therefore had to present them with the matching report that gave them detailed evidence of how and why we would be suitable parents to our girls and how we would meet their needs.

We were given a date and time for matching panel which was in the September, four months after we had been approved as adoptive parents and just less than two months after we had been matched with our girls.

I know we had been nervous at every stage of our Adoption Journey, especially at Approval Panel: however today topped it all! We were so close to becoming parents to two such amazing and beautiful baby girls who already felt like our daughters and we had dreams of our future together as a family. They were all that we had ever wanted in our lives and we already loved them so very much, even before we had even met them. We felt we knew every little detail about them, all of their little ways and we had watched them for hours on their

DVD and had their photographs all around our house BUT - what if the unthinkable happened? - and this panel of people sitting on the Matching Panel for some reason didn't recommend that we were a suitable match to be parents to our baby girls?

We were therefore more nervous and anxious than we had ever been during our lives: the most important decision ever for us, the decision whether we would become Mummy and Daddy to our babies was in the hands of this panel once again.

We had to just hope and pray that they would recommend us. We had provided all of the evidence that we possibly could, together with our social worker and the girls' social worker as to why and how we would be suitable parents. The decision was now down to the Matching Panel.

On the way to Panel, we stopped off at a supermarket for a coffee as once again we were very early. I was drawn to the children's clothes section and saw some gorgeous dresses for the girls. You get to a point when shopping, that all you can think about is things for the children, but, not wanting to tempt fate, we decided that we wouldn't buy them but would stop off on the way home and buy them if we were approved at Matching Panel.

We headed off for the remainder of the journey to the Social Services offices where the Matching Panel was being held. We went in and signed the attendance sheet, hardly able to hold the pen for shaking with nerves and we were then led into a waiting room where we met our social worker and the girls' social worker. We chatted for a short while before our social workers were asked into the Matching Panel to answer and clarify any questions that the Panel had for them before we were invited in.

The Panel Members introduced themselves and asked us a few questions: these were about how we would deal with certain situations, e.g. our girls were quite small for their age and we were tall people, so they wanted to know how we felt about this and how we may deal with it if people passed comments. They seemed easy questions for us to answer and we were able to reply to them honestly and in good detail and, fortunately, they all seemed very happy with our responses to the questions.

We then were asked to leave the room again whilst they voted and a few minutes later our Social Worker and The Adoption Manager returned to give us the news. It was a UNANIMOUS YES!! The news was magical, we would now be Mummy and Daddy to our beautiful daughters - we were so overjoyed and emotional.

We sat down with the social workers and made some dates as to how we would proceed with the Life Appreciation day and Introductions with our babies. Before we could begin Introductions we had to wait for the approval of the Agency Decision Maker again as you do at Adoption Approval Panel, because he has the power to make it official. We were told we should receive a letter from him in about a week's time and therefore had to arrange the dates for after we had received that letter.

We drove home so excited, trying to let everything sink in and pinching ourselves to make sure it wasn't all a dream. We were over the moon! We stopped back off at the shop on the way home and bought all of the gorgeous outfits that we had seen for our girls and it was from here that we rang our parents to let them know that they would be Grandparents very soon to our beautiful daughters.

Preparing For Our Babies

We had less than two weeks from the approval at Matching Panel to when we were to start Introductions with our babies. Most people have nine months to prepare for their babies' arrival, we had less than two weeks to buy equipment and get everything ready for our little girls, as you are advised not to get things until after you have been officially and successfully approved at Matching Panel.

Luckily we had decorated their bedrooms in neutral colours and had already had new carpets fitted prior to matching panel. Daddy had painted a beautiful jungle scene on one of the bedroom walls for our youngest and, as we had learnt that our eldest liked In 'The Night Garden', we had decorated her room with pictures of her favourite characters.

We had already purchased the two cot beds, the pushchairs and car seats before Matching Panel. We did wonder if we were doing the right thing as we didn't want to jinx anything, but when you look around shops and see that there is up to six weeks wait for items to come into stock and be delivered, we could foresee problems. We couldn't risk our things not arriving in time for our babies, so we took the decision to purchase the big items before matching panel.

There was, however, still an immense amount of items to buy so we made lots of lists of absolutely everything from nappies, wipes and bubble bath to clothes, toys and food and everything in between. We then went on some mammoth shopping trips and bought everything we could possibly need. It was a very hectic time but it was also such a lovely time to eventually be able to buy everything new for our baby girls who we knew would be coming home to us forever so very soon. It was also good to keep us busy and fill the time between being matched and meeting our daughters and starting Introductions.

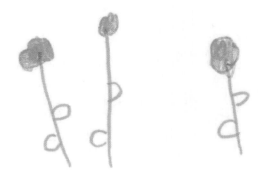

Preparation Books

We needed to make some age - appropriate resources for our girls so that we could help to prepare them for us being their Mummy and Daddy. At 9 months and 2 years old our girls obviously needed to be prepared for this massive event in their lives: they were having a Forever Mummy and Daddy who they had never met before in their lives.

We, as adults, obviously understood everything that was happening and had been given such detailed information about the girls, also seeing their pictures and films.

They, however, had no idea of the events in their lives that were about to happen so it was vital that we prepared them as best as we possibly could to help them understand in the simplest and kindest way possible, that we were going to be their Mummy and Daddy Forever and they would be coming to their Forever House.

We decided to make a talking photo album. These can be bought from large toy shops. They are very child friendly and made of strong, bright coloured plastic - ours was shaped like a butterfly. You put a photograph on each page and can do a different voice recording to go with each photograph coupled with a lovely twinkling sound as you turn each page.

We found this to be perfect so we did a picture of ourselves to begin with and did a recording to say "Hello (our girls names) we are going to be your Mummy and Daddy". We then did photos of the house, the garden, the local park, our car, etc. We took it in turns to do the voice recordings for each of the pages, so the girls could get used to hearing us, whilst at the same time familiarising themselves with their new home and environment.

We also made a more detailed photo book using an A4 scrap book, filling it with lots of photos and decorating each page with sparkly stickers. We used an Iggle Piggle cuddly toy and took each photograph with him in it, as our eldest liked this character. We even took Iggle Piggle to the park and photographed him on the slide and swings so the girls could see their local park.

I remember the morning that we did this very well; just as we started taking the photos at the park, the local football team arrived for their football training and there was me, my husband and Iggle Piggle on the park with no children in sight!, We did get some funny looks but we didn't care!

We took pictures of Iggle Piggle in their cots too, along with the cuddly rabbits that we had bought for them and these cuddlies would be waiting in their cots for them for when they arrived at their Forever Home.

Informing Work

The next job was to inform my work that I would be leaving in a few days! They obviously knew that we were adopting and were going to Matching Panel but nothing could be done officially with regards to my work until we had been successful at Matching Panel.

So now we had less than two weeks until the beginning of Introductions with our babies so work got very little notice. I also wanted to have a few days off before we began introductions to get everything ready for our girls so I went to see my manager and informed her that I would like to finish the following week to take a year's adoption leave. Her face was a picture! But she was very understanding and supportive and, as I worked for the NHS, they had policies in place for Adoption Leave which stated that you had to give them as much notice as was possible which, in my case, was a week, which they had to accept.

I was so excited about my final few days at work and was definitely on countdown as every day completed was a day nearer to meeting our babies.

I feel it important to mention that throughout the Adoption Process you will need to take a considerable number of days off work for social worker visits, the four day long Adoption Preparation Group, Adoption Panel, Matching Panel, meeting your children's foster carers, The Life Appreciation Day and then obviously Introductions so, if at all possible, it's a good idea to make sure you have lots of Annual Leave days saved up…. and an understanding manager really helps!

Life Appreciation Day

As we had now received the official letter, from the Agency Decision Maker, that we were approved as parents to our little girls, we were able to have the Life Appreciation Day. This is a day when all of the professionals that have ever had contact or input with our girls whilst in the birth family and foster care come together to celebrate and talk about their lives so far.

Each person who has worked with our girls has the opportunity to do a speech or presentation about their involvement and share the memories they have about our babies. By doing this it provided us with more information and details of our girls and what they had been through and done in their little lives so far, with personal accounts from the professionals who had been so closely involved in their life journey from the day that they were born until the present day. These professionals included their Health Visitor, Family Support Workers, Social Workers, Foster Carers and Contact Support Workers.

We really valued this day as it gave us a more detailed insight into all the involvement these professionals had with our girls and little snippets about our babies so we could understand more about them and their early lives. These professionals had been there and witnessed things first hand and could extend on the information we had read in the reports and they also answered all of our questions.

It was however very emotional and sad, as a lot of the negative events in their lives were highlighted by these professionals who had been involved on a day - to - day level with our girls and their birth parents.

The Life Appreciation Day was held in a Social Services Sure Start building. As we went into the allocated room we saw they had decorated it with enlarged photographs of our girls from birth until the present day. It was so lovely to be able to see their little faces on the photos, everywhere we looked.

We spent the whole day listening to short accounts of our girls, which enabled us to gain a better understanding of everything they done or had been through so far. We also held a detailed planning meeting to discuss how we were going to do Introductions: what time and for how long we would see our girls on each of the days during introductions and also the number of days Introductions would be spread over.

The next day we were going to be meeting our babies for the FIRST TIME! We were so excited and couldn't wait for 'tomorrow' to arrive.

After the Life Appreciation Day, the girls' social worker offered to show us the house that our eldest lived in before being taken into care. The social worker came in our car and directed us down a few streets to the house. This made me feel quite emotional, but I also took comfort in seeing the house and street where our baby once lived.

Being in an area that she had once been in felt important in the sense that we could see a place that she had lived before we became a Forever Family. To have knowledge of what this was like, was also helpful so that we can share it with her in the future, and could even show her if she wants to know.

This will help in her Life Story Work, helping her to gain a sense of her early days. I guess any parents like to know everything about their children and this was especially important as we didn't have the privilege of being with our babies from the day that they were born.

Meeting Our Beautiful Baby Girls

Introductions Day One

We had planned that today we would go to meet our babies for the first time at their foster home. We awoke early after struggling to sleep at all through excitement. We were eventually going to see our beautiful daughters for the first time; the most emotional and happy day of our lives was here at last!

We had arranged to arrive at the foster carers' house at 11am and stay for an hour. There were so many thoughts going through our heads on the long journey to see them. How would they react when they see us? Would they accept us or run (crawl!) the other way? No words could begin to describe the excitement and emotion that we were feeling to finally be able to meet our little girls.

We arrived and knocked on the front door and one of the foster carers' sons opened the door and let us in, leading us to the lounge where our girls were with the foster carer and their social worker.

We excitedly walked in and there they were in front of us, so delicate and beautiful. Our eldest little girl looked at us and smiled a great big smile and our baby was sat on the floor gazing up at us.

The foster carer said, "Who's this?" to which our eldest daughter replied, "Mummy and Daddy". I tried my hardest to fight back the tears of joy, not wanting to let them see me crying, but I failed and happy tears were welling up in my eyes. I cannot begin to put the emotion into words of how we felt seeing our babies for the first time, there in front of us were our precious little daughters, so beautiful and perfect in every way. I really wanted to scoop them up, and give them both kisses and cuddles, but held back as I knew that this wouldn't be fair on them.

Although we knew we were Mummy and Daddy, to them at this moment we were just two strange adults who they had never met before. Did they really understand what Mummy and Daddy meant at 9 months old and just 2 years old, when they had never known what a Mummy and Daddy was? Realistically it was probably just a word to our eldest although it sounded so lovely when she called it us, but we didn't want to overwhelm them at first with giving them lots of hugs and kisses until they were comfortable with us.

We therefore needed to gain their trust, love and acceptance and help them to understand what a Mummy and Daddy were and what this meant and to help them trust and believe that we were going to be there to love and cherish them and meet all of their needs forever and ever.

Having said all that, it was as though our eldest somehow just KNEW that we were her Mummy and Daddy, something the foster carer and social worker also commented on. It was as if she was just waiting for her own Mummy and Daddy and could sense that we had arrived for her.

She sat there on the sofa holding the photo book that we had made for them, looking at the pictures and then pointing at us as if she was making the connection between the photographs and ourselves. The foster carer commented that she hadn't put the book down since she had given it to her the previous night. Due to a problem with the girls' social worker getting the book to them, they had only been given it the night before we arrived after the Life Appreciation Day. This was far from ideal at all, as children should be prepared gradually over at least a week when they are this age. However, even though she had only just been given it the night before, she did seem to somehow be understanding.

Our baby was a bit more wary of us at first. Only being 9 months old she obviously had no proper understanding of who we were or what was happening but she soon came around and began accepting us too, crawling around the room and coming over to us every so often and sitting on our knees and playing.

We gave the girls our undivided attention for the full hour, playing and interacting together. After a few minutes of us arriving the foster carers and social workers went in the other room to leave us to play, bond and interact with our babies which was thoughtful. We had a wonderful time with our girls and it was definitely the fastest hour ever; we wanted to freeze time and never leave our babies' sides. We understood that the first visit was planned to just last one hour, so as not to overwhelm our girls at the beginning but we loved them so much and wished we never had to leave them.

When we did have to leave it was so hard to say goodbye; we had just met our beautiful girls and now we were having to say "Goodbye" for the day. We gave our girls a little kiss before saying our goodbyes and they responded well to our affection. It was such a wonderful experience to kiss our babies' soft skin for the first time, a very special memory.

Introductions Day Two

The plan today was to visit our girls from 11am until 2.30pm, at the foster carers' house so that we could incorporate giving our girls their lunch during our visit. This was so we could get used to mealtimes and the girls could get used to us feeding them and being with them while they were having a meal.

We arrived at 11 am and the girls both seemed really pleased to see us which was a huge relief. They were very eager to play and interact with us which was lovely and a sign that they were beginning to accept us and be comfortable in our company.

We had another wonderful time playing and building numerous towers for the girls out of mega blocks which our eldest especially loved to knock down, and she would then hand us the bricks for us to rebuild another tower. This was by far her favourite game and she loved it and laughed so much when she knocked the tower over. We loved it too, just hearing her laughing and seeing her beautiful smile: this was a really wonderful early bonding experience.

At lunch time we gave them a sandwich and it amazed us how much our baby could eat with only having half a tooth! They sat in their highchairs munching away, smiling and babbling with us as they ate. It was however quite a strange experience doing the lunchtime routine in the foster carer's house. It was like feeding our children in a stranger's house and although she was really accommodating and let us get on with everything, the programme of introductions in another person's house is a surreal experience.

You want to do everything for your children and take care of their every need but then find yourself asking if it's ok to make up a bottle, or get some more clothes out of their wardrobe, trying to fit in with how other people do things while in their house.

We took our own changing bag, nappies, bottles, bibs and even some clothes during the introductions as we felt that in a few days we would properly be Mummy and Daddy in our own house and surroundings and would then be using all of our own things, so we thought we should be prepared from the start. We also wanted to show that we didn't need to rely on the foster carers for everything and that we were organised and competent.

We asked the foster carer what type of washing powder she used prior to introductions so that we could wash the girls' clothes and bedding in the same powder to begin with so even their things smelt of a familiar smell.

This was important as our girls were having so many new experiences and such a big change in their lives, we wanted to let them have as much comfort as possible from little things that were familiar to them, especially as children are very sensitive to smells.

I have a very special memory the week prior to introductions when I was longing see our girls, not being able to take my mind off them for a second and wanting to feel like Mummy, doing things for them even before meeting them so I washed all of their brand spanking new clothes.

This gave me comfort and satisfaction that I was preparing everything for their arrival and gave me something constructive to do with my time. All I could think about was our babies and the time prior to introductions seemed to go so slowly as we were so desperate to meet our girls.

Our washing line looked so beautiful, full of their little pink outfits all blowing in the wind; it was the only time that I had time to iron everything so perfectly too, even the socks!

After we had given the girls their dinner it was time to clean them up, change them and put them into their cots for their nap, wanting to stick rigidly to their routine.

The time had flown again and we really didn't want to have to say 'Bye Bye" to them, but we knew that we had to adhere to the introductions plan so even though it was hard to leave them for the rest of the day we had no other option.

We tucked them into their cots for their nap and said "Goodbye", explaining that we would see them again tomorrow - not that they understood what we were saying at such a young age- but it felt right.

We could feel a real sense of an amazing bond building between all of us. The girls stayed very close to us for the whole of our visit and interacted really well with us. We could tell that they were really relaxed and enjoying our company and all of the attention that we were giving them.

Again, leaving them was so hard as we just wanted to be with them and wanted them to be with us, their Mummy and Daddy. It felt so wrong to be leaving our girls at the foster carers' house and returning home on our own but we understood that introductions needed to be taken slowly and gradually for our girls' sake to help them to adjust and trust us, so they could feel safe and secure.

When we got home, I went straight up to their bedrooms, looking at their empty little cots and just longing for the day that they would be home with us and we would be putting them to bed in their own cots in our Forever Home rather than at the foster carers' house.

Introductions Day Three

Today we had planned to be with our girls for the afternoon and do the tea, bath and bedtime routine with them. We arrived at 3pm and the plan was to stay until we had put our babies to bed at around 7pm- that is if we had managed to do all of these things for the first time and get them into bed by 7pm!

The girls were both really pleased to see us again and of course we were so excited to see them and we played together endlessly. We had arranged with the foster carer to take them to the park for an hour before tea. They were really beginning to trust us and were happy in our company so we thought that they would be ready for our first little trip out together.

We got them ready, a task that takes much longer than you anticipate with two little ones; we changed their nappies and got them ready in their little jackets and shoes. Just as we thought we were finally ready, our baby filled her nappy! So we very carefully changed her nappy as new parents do, treating her like she was so fragile and delicate that we hardly dared lift her legs. It must have taken us a good ten minutes and then we had to work out all of the poppers on the vests and try to dress her, afraid to bend her arms too much to get them back into the sleeve holes.

Then just as we thought we were ready again our eldest didn't want to miss out and she too needed a nappy change!

Eventually we were ready to head for the car and strapped them into their brand new car seats for the first time, very nervously checking and double checking that they were in comfortably and securely. I must say I am glad that we practised beforehand, although it's never the same practising with empty car seats, but our babies were so good, they must have known that we were new to this and were very patient with us whilst we strapped them in.

We drove the short distance to the park, remembering the directions from the foster carer in this unfamiliar town. We arrived and our eldest was very eager to play on all the play things.

Soon after arriving she took a tumble as she was running around and I felt like a really bad parent and so guilty that she had fallen over, even though this obviously wasn't my fault. I somehow thought that I should have anticipated this and been able to catch her before she hit the ground. Luckily she was fine and didn't even have a graze, just tripping over her own feet and bouncing straight up - but it didn't stop me from wanting to wrap her in cotton wool to protect her.

We played on the play equipment and all had a brilliant time together on our first fabulous little family outing- a day we will never forget. Before long though it was time to return to the foster carers for tea.

We arrived back and got the girls ready for their tea which the foster carer had kindly prepared. Her family sat around the table and we sat at the edge with our girls in their highchairs and fed them their meal which they ate beautifully.

We then ran the girls' bath and I became paranoid about the bath temperature, repeatedly checking it with my elbow to ensure it wasn't too hot for their delicate skin. They loved their bath and had fun splashing around and I very carefully washed their hair to ensure that I didn't get any water in their eyes in case they never forgave me!

Luckily bathtime went really well and we washed their hair without any tears. We got them out and Daddy and I each dried one of our babies, trying to do it quickly so they didn't get cold but knowing that this was the first time we had done this and appreciated that we were probably actually going at a very slow pace. The house was very warm so fortunately this wasn't a problem and we dressed the girls in their sleepsuits and dried and brushed their hair carefully.

We took the girls to their cots following the routine that they had established with the foster carers, to try and ensure that we kept everything as consistent as possible for them. We tucked them into their cots and they both screamed, we comforted them but every time we went to leave the room they became really upset.

The foster carer came up and told us that they do this and that we should just shut the door and leave them to cry and eventually they will cry themselves to sleep! We weren't keen on doing this but we appreciated that we were in somebody else's house with their routines and ways of doing things, but it was *our* children who were involved. We would do things differently but we acknowledged that we couldn't change this overnight and, probably more importantly, in somebody else's house. So we kissed our babies goodnight and had no other option but to leave them there crying.

It was heart wrenching leaving our girls at the foster carer's for the night, knowing that they were so upset, leaving our babies screaming in somebody else's house and having to leave when all that we wanted was for our babies to be with us so that we could love, cuddle and cherish them.

We took comfort however, knowing that we had less than 12 hours until we would be with them again. It was 7.30pm and the plan was that tomorrow we would arrive at 7am to get our babies up out of their cots and do the morning routine with them. We were staying in a hotel tonight nearby as we had an early morning and the 120 mile round trip was quite tiring. We had some tea at the hotel and went to bed for an early night. Introductions are truly amazing but they are very emotionally and physically intense so we were ready for an early night.

I lay in bed thinking and hoping that our babies were settled and fast asleep; I couldn't bear to think of them still crying when we couldn't be there to comfort them. I then had a mad panic, - I had forgotten to brush their teeth. Bad Mummy moment, especially as I thought that we had done so well with the bedtime routine! I wondered whether to phone the foster carer but then thought there was no point as she wasn't going to wake them up at 10pm to clean their teeth but it didn't stop me from feeling guilty.

Introductions Day Four

We arrived at the foster carers' house bright and early at 7am, as planned, and our girls were already awake, they were thrilled to see us and obviously we were to see them too.

The plan today was to spend the whole day with our babies and take them out to the park, a Soft Play Centre and have lunch out. We gave the girls their breakfast and then got them dressed and, after a little play at the foster carers' house, we got them ready for our outing.

I think that I had packed enough things to last us a week but you never know, as a new parent, how much you will need and how many changes of clothes the girls would get through so we were prepared for every eventuality.

I got the bottles ready and filled them with boiled water, and had a container with the formula milk in so that we could just add the powder to the bottles as and when we needed them. Doing it this way meant that the bottles would be fresh, as we weren't going to have a fridge. Out of the fridge if the bottles are already made up, they have to be used within an hour.

We were much faster today getting the girls ready then drove to the park. We arrived, got the girls into their brand new, squeaky clean pushchairs for the first time. They looked very comfortable, we went for a lovely walk and had a play on the park which delighted the girls.

Then we headed to the soft play and had an amazing day out as our little family. The girls relished the soft play (as did we!), our baby was pulling herself up and walking around all of the soft play mats. We were so proud of her, at only 9 months, but, behind her every step of the way, we were there ready to catch her if she wobbled. We didn't need to worry though, she was so strong and determined and was so happy pottering around, playing peek-a-boo with us from behind the soft play shapes.

Our eldest was racing around so excited, it was a joy to see her so happy and she loved playing in the ball pool with us. They both seemed so relaxed and content in our company and we all had so much fun playing and interacting together as a proper little family at last. Our dreams were now a reality!

We had lunch together at the soft play centre and before long our baby fell fast asleep in her pushchair, her busy play session having worn her out! I couldn't take my eyes off her, lying there fast asleep looking so cute and content. Our eldest however was still full of endless energy and, after dinner, was ready for another play. Daddy and I took it in turns to play on the soft play with her whilst the other was sat next to our sleeping baby girl. The time had flown by again and after a fabulous day out - the first time that we had spent the whole day out together as a family- we had to return to the foster carers' house, taking with us our special memories of today.

We got the girls ready for their tea and then had to leave them with the foster carers as today's plan was to be with them from 7am until 4pm. The girls didn't want us to leave them and it was so hard for us having to leave them there upset; we had to kiss them goodbye and then waved at them as they cried for us.

It was heart - breaking but at least we knew that it was getting closer to the day that our girls would come and live with us forever. We just wished that they could understand this as we felt so cruel leaving them at the foster carers, so upset but not being of an age to understand why we were having to leave them at the end of each day.

Tomorrow was the day that our girls would come to our house for the first time for a visit and a play. They would see their Forever Home and we were so excited. It was arranged that the foster carers would bring them to our house and they would all stay for an hour before the foster carers took our girls back to their house.

We arrived home and I began frantically cleaning the house ready for our babies' arrival the next day. The house was already clean but I wanted it spotless for them (not that they would notice or even care in the slightest!) but I did it anyway. I can only compare it to when nesting instincts kick in for people having a baby and everything has to be just perfect for the new arrivals.

House sparkling clean, I began the exciting task of bringing all of the girls' new toys down for the very first time - they had been sat in the girls' new bedrooms waiting for this day. I began the task of trying to extract all of the packaging off the new toys and then set them all up in the lounge which was beginning to resemble an over - stocked toy shop!

I wanted the girls to see that their new home was a happy and inviting place where they could relax and have endless fun, with all the love and affection that they could possibly have from their doting Mummy and Daddy.

A quick dash to the supermarket to stock up on fruit, snacks and all of their favourite foods. Although they were only coming for an hour I wanted the cupboards full, just in case!

Introductions Day 5

We woke up early, so excited about our babies coming to see us and their new house for the first time. I prepared juice, sterilised the bottles and got some snacks ready for them. We sat looking at their toys, longing for them to arrive at their Forever Home. I think I must have been looking out of the window, wishing for them to arrive from about 8 am, although they weren't due until 11am. I somehow convinced myself that they may just be early- but they weren't!

Just after 11am and the foster carers' car pulled up outside with our beautiful babies in the back. We rushed to open the door and went out to greet them and give them a big cuddle and brought them into their Forever House.

They straight away began playing happily with us and all of their new toys. We had a great time and it was so nice for us all to be at home together. I think they somehow must have sensed that this was home as they were so content and happy in what was an unfamiliar place for them.

The foster carers weren't in a rush and were happy to let the girls have lunch with us. They had sandwiches, fruit and yoghurt with us which they ate beautifully in their new highchairs and it was SO lovely to have our first lunchtime together at our house.

After lunch the foster carers had to take the girls back to their house. It was another very hard and emotional experience, waving goodbye to our babies as they got back into the foster carers' car for their journey back.

We were so happy to have had our babies at home with us and then after a couple of hours they had to go back with the foster carers but we understood that everything needs to be done gradually in introductions but it doesn't help the emotions of your precious babies having to be taken away again.

We were relieved at how well everything had gone and that the girls were happy and relaxed in their new home and surroundings, and even more so, were happy with us!

Introductions Day 6

Today it had been planned that the foster carers would bring our girls to our house again but they would just drop them off with us. They would go out for lunch, leaving the girls with us for their lunch and we would have an afternoon playing together.

Again they arrived at 11am and, after a morning waiting for their arrival and envisaging where they may be on their journey every few minutes, we saw them pull up outside.

They eagerly came in and were really pleased to see us again, as we were them. The foster carers left and the girls weren't fazed in the slightest. They were both so happy and we were relieved that our babies were relaxed and content to be with us again. They obviously trusted us and felt all the love that we had for them.

We played for the whole time, giving the girls our undivided attention and they enjoyed everything that we did and were happy and smiley. We had bought them a new play kitchen, our eldest had endless fun pretending to make us drinks, whilst our baby pulled herself up and walked around it, emptying everything off the kitchen that her sister had put on. They both loved every minute.

We had a brief stop for lunch and then continued the fun all afternoon until the foster carers arrived back to take our babies on the journey back to their house. Our eldest cried at having to leave us. It was extremely heart - warming that they were so happy with us and wanted to stay but so sad to see them leaving with the foster carers. Our eldest little girl was so upset and we couldn't be there to hug and comfort her.

The foster carer sent us a message on her journey back, that our eldest girlie had buried her head in her coat and refused to look at, or speak to the foster carer for the whole two hour journey back.

It was lovely to hear that she wanted us and that she was annoyed with the foster carer for taking her away from us. However, it was so upsetting that evening knowing that she had been so distressed and confused, wondering and hoping that she was ok and settled now. We were wishing for the time to speed up so that we could be with our gorgeous girls again.

Introductions Day 7

The social workers, ourselves and the foster carers had a review meeting to discuss how everything was going. It was decided that introductions needed to be speeded up as it was going so successfully. The girls were bonding with us so well that they were actually getting distressed about leaving us at the end of each day, especially our eldest little girl who had more understanding due to her age.

Everyone was in agreement that it was in our girls' best interests for them to come and live with us forever sooner than originally planned, so the date was set for Wednesday 22nd September. Hooray - only two days away! We were so excited that we finally had a definite date that our little daughters were coming home to live with us as a Forever Family.

We collected our babies from the foster carers at 10am as planned. Today we were going to bring them back to our house for the day and then have tea together and bath them at our house, then take them the 60 mile journey back to the foster carers' house for bedtime.

Our girls were so good with all of the travelling. It was such a long time for them in the car but they were happy and content to listen to me singing nursery rhymes (poor girls!) and generally chatting about anything and everything.

I packed lots of little toys for them to play with whilst sitting in their car seats and our eldest loved looking through picture books and having stories, whilst our cheeky baby had endless fun throwing her rattles on the floor for me to squirm and reach behind the back seats for, doing her cheeky little giggle, (yes little one, you have always been a cheeky little bundle of fun X).

Our baby cooed and babbled, happily smiling in response to peek -a -boo and our little games. It was an ideal opportunity to begin to teach our eldest little girl some new words and help her extend her vocabulary. She was able to say Mummy, Daddy and her sister's name, but we were keen to help her learn new words and give her new experiences and opportunities. We constantly chatted, teaching her all of the animal names as we drove past them in the beautiful countryside on the way home.

She amazed us at how quickly she was learning all of the animal names and the noises that each animal made. She was such a clever little girl and it became apparent that she just needed the time, attention and stimulation to enable her to develop to her full potential. We were also amazed at our baby's ability, when we mentioned the word 'pig', she suddenly began making snorting sounds. She had probably heard us do it fifty times during the journey but we were still astonished that at only 9 months old, she was understanding and responding to us so well. This was the first proper animal sound that she made, and each time we saw a pig she recognised it and did her little piggy noise. It was so cute and clever for a baby of only 9 months old and we were such proud parents of our little girls.

We arrived home at our house and the girls were instantly happy and content to be at home with us; we all had amazing fun again and a really happy time playing together. Again their favourite toy was their kitchen and our eldest girlie made us pretend cups of tea and pressed all of the buttons to make the little noises on the kitchen. Our baby would pull herself up on anything and everything and walk around holding onto the furniture and window sills. Today was the first time that she had crawled properly, previously she had commando crawled on her knees and forearms. Another proud Mummy and Daddy moment!

Before we knew it teatime had arrived. I put the shepherd's pie that I had prepared the previous evening into the oven to cook, proud of myself for being organised and already having a meal prepared so that we could spend all afternoon with our girls.

We put the girls into their highchairs and gave them their tea. We soon discovered that shepherd's pie was not a hit, our baby had a few spoonsful and our eldest refused it altogether. Eventually with much encouragement she had a couple of spoonsful but the fruit and yoghurt went down much better.

Time for their first bath at home and they loved it. With all of their new bath toys, there was hardly room for them, but they had great fun playing and splashing around in the water. Their beautiful baby clean smell when we got them out was gorgeous and we wrapped them in their new fluffy hooded towels to keep them cosy before dressing them in their soft new sleep suits. We brushed their teeth, although our youngest only had half a tooth and she had more fun trying to knaw on the toothbrush.

I prepared their bottles of milk and wrapped them in their pink fleecy blankets before putting them into their car seats for the journey back to the foster carers' house. They were both fast asleep within half an hour and I spent the rest of the journey gazing at our beautiful, peaceful babies as they slept contently in the back of the car.

They slept for the whole journey and were still asleep when we pulled up at the foster carers' house, but as we got them out of the car and carried them in, they both awoke. They both also cried as we had to leave again - another very emotional and painful experience to leave our babies crying as we had to head back home without them.

The journey home was very hard again, to drive back, just the two of us when we were a family of four now, their little car seats empty. All we wanted was for them to be in there with us and we were really hoping that they were ok now and had stopped crying.

It was getting very late when we eventually arrived home and we were tired after the 240 miles that we had travelled in addition to an emotionally intense day with our beautiful girls, so we headed to bed so that we could be full of energy ready for our day with our babies again tomorrow.

Introductions Day 8

Today was an exciting early start as we were going to arrive at the foster carers' house at 7am. We got up at 4.30am and set off on the journey to see our babies, hoping to be there in time for when they woke up.

Throughout the Introduction period, you spend lots of full days out with your babies which is absolutely amazing and a very special time. It can also be quite tricky though in the sense that you are basically living out of your extremely large handbag, changing bag and car, when out and about with your babies.

When people have a new baby and they are getting used to becoming parents, they are normally at home, with everything that they could possibly need around them. They may go on short trips out, but are based from their comfortable home environment.

When adopting and during Introductions, you have to be very organised and plan each day thoroughly to ensure that you have everything that you and your babies will need. You are either in a stranger's (foster carers') house, or you are taking your children out for the day; in our case this was exaggerated further because of the distance from where we lived to where our babies were in foster care.

It means that you need to bond and get to know your babies, meeting their needs and maintaining their routines as much as possible, whilst spending large portions of the day away from the home environment.

Mealtimes, sleep times and changing etc. therefore require lots of forward planning. Even negotiating the café with two young babies in pushchairs, getting them in and out of highchairs and finding somewhere to prepare and warm their milk in unfamiliar places is quite testing for a new parent.

Fortunately we had a very large car boot, so this became the changing station, and we could fit a 'mini nursery' into it, to ensure that we had everything we needed when out for such long periods each day. The pushchairs were very useful for their sleep times when we didn't have their cots to use.

We had a good journey on the way to see our babies as there was very little traffic on the roads at this time in the morning. We arrived at their house just before 7am and rushed in to see them. They were still in their cots so we went straight upstairs. They were both awake sitting in their cots as we peeped round the door and their little faces lit up when we walked into the bedroom that they shared together. Our girls were thrilled to see us, as we were them and we picked them up and had big, squidgy cuddles – so, so beautiful and special!

We took the girls downstairs and gave them their breakfast and then got them dressed, keeping to their normal routine. Today we were going to take the girls out for the day, staying local to where the foster carers lived. We were very conscious that the long journeys back to our house were not ideal for the girls to keep having to endure. Although they had been so good travelling, we didn't think that it was fair for them to have to be in the car again for another 4 hours today. We therefore decided to take them out to a nice park and then out for lunch and we were lucky that the weather was being kind to us and it was a lovely sunny day.

Again I had packed the car full of everything we could possibly need, resembling the amount of things you would probably take for a weekend away but taking comfort in knowing that every eventuality was prepared for.

We had a lovely play on the park and just enjoyed being with the girls and feeling like a proper little family, we then found a nice pub for lunch. After lunch we got in a proper little mess with very drippy ice-creams which the girls loved! We settled them down in their pushchairs for their afternoon naps and had a lovely stroll around the pretty villages whilst the girls slept peacefully in their pushchairs as we proudly pushed them around.

This was our final day of introductions as tomorrow our babies would be coming home forever. We were so excited! If only our two beautiful, cute little sleeping babies knew that tomorrow they would be with Mummy and Daddy Forever and ever. They both looked so content having their little naps in their new but not so sparkly clean pushchairs now they had shared their ice creams with the pushchairs!

We headed back to the foster carers' house for 4pm, so relieved that this was our final time of having to say goodbye to our babies and leave them at the foster carers'; it's such a hard thing to do. They were our babies now and we already felt like a proper little family, but then we had to take them back each evening and say goodbye as they cried at the door.... a really traumatic and surreal experience.

We took them into the foster carers' house and gave them both big loves before saying goodbye. Again they both cried when we went to leave and our eldest put her arms up to us. We really didn't want to leave them and knew that we had no choice, but all we wanted to do was to scoop them up and take them home with us. We said goodbye and just wished they could understand that tomorrow they would be with us forever and ever and we would never have to say goodbye to them again.

The foster carers had a couple of bags containing a few clothes and toys that they wanted us to take today as it would be too emotional for them tomorrow with having to say goodbye to the girls.

We drove home longing for it to be tomorrow so we could collect our baby girls. We arrived home and I did a quick dash to the supermarket to fill the cupboards in preparation for our babies' arrival. The last thing I wanted was to have to go shopping once our babies were home, as I wanted to spend the first few days solely with them, without having to go out and do the food shopping.

Wednesday 22nd September- The Best Day Of Our Lives

Bringing Our Babies Home Forever xxxx

Today was the day that we had always longed for, our babies coming home FOREVER! Words cannot express how overjoyed and excited we were.

We set off at 7am on the car journey to collect our babies, arriving as planned at the foster carers' house for 9.15am. We walked into the house and there waiting for us were our beautiful girlies. We scooped them up and gave them big cuddles and they were beaming at us, so happy to see us too. The foster carer had already said that she didn't want emotional goodbyes and had asked us to just collect the girls as quickly as possible.

It was obviously a very emotional time for everybody and although for us it was such an amazingly happy day, we couldn't help but feel sorry for the foster carers that they had to say goodbye to our baby girls.

We carried our girls out to the car, saying a quick goodbye and a very big thank you to the foster carers, leaving them a present as a thank you in the kitchen.

We walked to the car with our gorgeous girls in our arms. They were smiling and happy and seemed as excited and overjoyed as we were. We strapped our babies into their car seats and the foster carers' social worker came out to the car with us. The foster carers stayed in the house, feeling too emotional to come out to wave goodbye.

Their social worker was a really lovely and caring older lady, she came out to the car with us and wished us all the very best. She said what brilliant parents she thought we were for our girls, which meant a lot to us, and then she wished us all a very happy life together.

We waved goodbye and set off on our journey back to our Forever Home, all of us together in our little family. We felt so excited and so lucky to be starting family life together, blessed with our two adorable little daughters who were just perfect in every way.

We chatted together all of the way home and I said to our babies that we were Mummy and Daddy now forever and ever, telling them how much we dearly loved them and how we would always be there for them to love and cherish them. I know they were too young to understand but I needed to tell them, and they both smiled in response as if somehow they just knew, bless them.

They were really happy and vocal on the journey home, our eldest girlie was trying her hardest to say little words and we were getting better at understanding her and our baby was cooing and happily babbling away. It was a really special journey, so lovely to know that we were all together forever now.

We arrived home and it was just as if they knew this was their home. They settled in so well and were so content and happy, bouncing around with endless energy. We showered them with love, affection and attention, playing constantly with them to help them understand that we would always meet their every need and they could rely on us for everything, the bond between us continuing to grow stronger and stronger.

The first night we hardly slept a wink, so nervous about dropping off to sleep in case they were crying and we didn't hear them. It soon became obvious that this wouldn't happen; there was no chance that we wouldn't hear them as they are very vocal and I became a very light sleeper anyway, hearing every little sound they made and dashing into them when they murmured.

It was very tiring though at first, as the days were so intense now and we were lucky if we found time to even sit and have a coffee.

I know the social workers told us to make the most of our sleep before our babies came home and we now realised what they meant- sleep would never be the same again!

As our daughters naturally don't need much sleep and wake continually through the night, we soon got used to surviving on the minimal amount of sleep, but didn't mind in the slightest. We have our babies and all that mattered now was them.

If felt so special knowing that our babies were now with us forever and being able to do all the normal family things with our girls which we had always wished for and making memories together to last a lifetime.

Our life is totally amazing! We have longed for this time for all of our lives; the day we finally had our babies and became a Forever Family. We feel so lucky to be Mummy and Daddy to our two such amazing, unique and beautiful baby girls who we love more than anything in the world- our life is now complete.

Changing Our Baby's Name

When children are adopted, they usually keep their original Christian names. Once you have the Adoption Order granted by the courts, the children will be officially given their adoptive parents' surname.

In some instances the adoptive parents are given permission to choose a middle name for their children to either be used alongside the child's previous middle name or by changing it altogether.

The child's 'new' surnames and middle names will be entered onto their Adoption Certificates. These are very similar to birth certificates and state the child's name, date of birth, place of birth and Adoptive Parents' names, address and occupations. They also state the date the adoption order was granted and by which court.

The Adoption Certificates are obtained from the General Register Office- the same as birth certificates are, and you use them exactly the same as you would birth certificates for official purposes, applying for passports etc.

We received our girls' Adoption Certificates in the post approximately two weeks after the courts had granted the Adoption Order. The courts provide all of the official paperwork and send it to the General Register Office to enable them to issue the Adoption Certificates.

It was another really special moment when we received our girls Adoption Certificates through the post, the 'icing on the cake' to have in front of us our girls' certificates with their new names and *us* named as Mummy and Daddy!

Our girls both had very unusual and unique first names, but our youngest especially. We were therefore told by the social services department that we needed to change her first name, because of how unusual it was, but also because of the reasons why she was named it. We could therefore choose a totally new name for her!

We were a bit shocked as we weren't expecting to be able to change her name, even though we knew how uncommon it was. After some long discussions, my husband and I decided on a name that we both loved. We informed the social workers who agreed that it was a beautiful name which really suited our baby girl.

Although thrilled and excited to have been given the special honour of being able to choose a name for our baby, like birth parents have the pleasure of doing when their baby is born, we were quite apprehensive about changing her name.

Her name was her little identity, it was who she had been for the first nine months of her life and we found it quite emotional to suddenly be taking a little part of her identity away and changing it.

We realised the importance of doing this though, both to protect her, her sister and our confidentiality and identity. This was also important so she didn't have to go through life explaining to people about her name and why she was called this, which would have created some unwanted questions for her.

We obviously loved her new name which we had been given the privilege of being able to choose for her, but we wanted to learn the best way of introducing her new name to her.

As our baby was only nine months old, she was only just beginning to recognise her original Christian name but we were concerned for our eldest daughter who had always known her sister by her original name. How would she react when we suddenly began calling her sister by a completely different name?

We took advice from the social workers about this, and our girls' social worker suggested that from the first day of Introductions, when we meet our girls we should call our baby by her new first name.

I wondered if we should somehow have incorporated her previous name and new name and called her by both, similar to a hyphenated name, until she and her sister began getting used to it, and recognising her by it, and then gradually dropping her previous name.

We did as we were advised though and began calling our baby by the name we had chosen for her straight away, and due to her young age, she accepted this and soon began responding to it when we spoke to her.

Our eldest however found this much more difficult, every time we said our baby's name she would say, "No, that is *****", trying to correct us.

I found it very upsetting for our eldest, she already had so many immense changes going on in her life; a new Mummy and Daddy, a new house, basically everything was different for her, and her one comfort- her familiar baby sister - was now being called by a strange name!

She continued to refer to her sister by her previous name, and we never tried to correct her, or told her that this was wrong, but we always called our baby her new name.

About two months after the girls came home forever, to our astonishment, our eldest began calling her sister by her new name. From this day onwards she has never called her sister by her previous name- not even once. It was as if she was ready, and secure enough to accept her sister's new name and in her own time was at a stage where she was able to do this.

The names couldn't be officially changed until we had been granted the Adoption Order in court, which was to happen six months after the girls came to live with us.
Therefore when we went to Doctors, Dentists, Health Visitor appointments, hospitals etc. she was still referred to by her previous names.

Some places were more accommodating than others about putting a note on their systems to request that she was referred to by her new names for both security and our eldest daughter's benefit, so not to confuse her by hearing her sister being called by different names.

Once we had the official Adoption Certificate, after the Adoption Order had been granted, we could officially change it with all the relevant places and departments which was nice.

We were able to choose new middle names for both of our daughters. This was really lovely, and enabled us to give both of our babies a name that we had chosen for them. This wasn't a problem for our eldest daughter, as although she was very aware of her Christian name and would have been upset and confused if we changed it, she wasn't aware of her original middle name, so changing it wasn't going to be distressing for her.

My husband and I decided that we would give both of our babies my middle name, so they both had a part of me and my identity.

Although sisters aren't usually given the same middle names, we considered it to be important for our girls to both have part of Mummy's name. We otherwise wouldn't have been able to decide which daughter to give part of Mummy's name to and felt that it was unfair to give it to one and not the other, so we came to the decision that it would be special for them both; and for Mummy too!

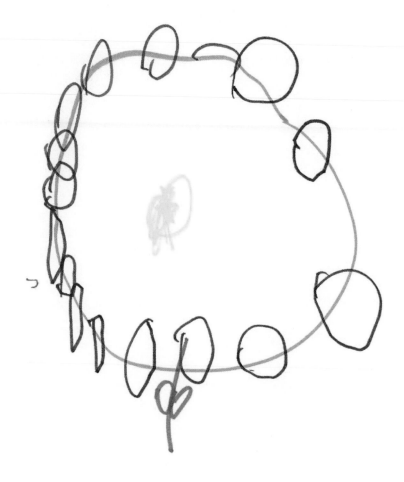

Introducing Our Babies To Family & Friends

Although very excited about introducing our babies to our family and friends, we felt that it was important that we didn't do this for at least a week, and then we would do it very gradually, so not to overwhelm the girls.

We decided to see how everything went and just enjoyed having our girls to ourselves, to love and bond with, but we were also conscious of how desperate the grandparents were to meet them. We also didn't want to keep people away for too long as this is not normal, to go for long periods of time without seeing anybody else. We decided that we would take things day by day and definitely not rush anything.

After a week we asked the grandparents if they would like to come around to see us at our house where the girls were settled. We thought this would be better than us taking the girls to the grandparents' houses that would have been strange and unfamiliar to them, with people (grandparents) who they had never met before and were strangers to them too. We thought that this may be frightening or unsettling for the girls so having the grandparents at our house, which was familiar to the girls, was the best option.

For the first visit we asked the grandparents to just come for a short visit so as not to overwhelm the girls, and for them to come at different times so both sets of grandparents were not here together, which again could have been too much for the girls to cope with.

It was lovely to finally let the grandparents meet our gorgeous girls and the girls were both ok, although a lot quieter and more suspicious and wary than when they were with us. This was a good response and showed that our babies were bonding successfully with us.

We gradually, over the next few weeks, introduced them to the rest of the family and our friends. We had to keep reminding ourselves that although we knew that all these people that were visiting were kind and caring people, for the girls they were all strangers who they had never met before and this could easily have been threatening for them. This is something that I will write about in greater depth further on.

Learning To Trust and Feel Safe & Secure

In all of the excitement for us of finally becoming a Forever Family with our two most beautiful babies, it was important to remember that our girls weren't born the day they came to our Forever Home, and that they had both not had the start in life that we would have wished for them. Although still only babies themselves, they have had to endure more suffering in their short little lives than most people do in a lifetime.

Most children are able to begin to bond and attach to their parents from the second that they are born and research has shown the importance of these early relationships on the social and emotional development of children.

As our baby girls have not been able to have this, we were only too aware of how important it was for them to be able to bond and attach to us from the day that we became Mummy and Daddy and for them to learn to understand that we can be trusted to provide them with everything they need.

By repeatedly meeting the girls' needs we will become a conditioned source of comfort, helping them to learn to regulate their own emotional arousal so they can trust us and feel secure and begin to attach successfully to us.

It has been impossible for our girls to have successfully attached to anyone in their past. They were removed from birth parents who had never been able to meet their basic needs, a social worker (who to them was a stranger) had taken them to the foster carers' house, who were two more strangers.

The foster family was very large and busy; they had five birth children as well as our two girls who they fostered, so it was very hard for them to successfully attach to a primary caregiver. They were then taken to two different respite foster carers on two occasions when their foster carers went on holidays, with no preparation, and again, to complete strangers in the girls' eyes.

They were also taken, by sometimes unfamiliar social workers and support workers to contact meetings with the birth parents, who they did not really know. The girls were too young to understand who they were and the birth parents had never met their needs.

This demonstrated to us what a scary little world our beautiful babies had lived in, never really knowing each day when they woke up who they would be with.

Would somebody come and pick them up and take them off to a different 'stranger's' house (respite foster carer) or be taken in a strange car by an unfamiliar person to a contact visit with the birth parents who were like strangers to them?

After the lives that they had lived, how could our innocent little babies ever begin to trust and properly believe that they would be with us, Mummy and Daddy, forever and ever without being separated from us? So far in their little lives, they had never had the security of this, so we knew that we had to do everything that we possibly could to help them to feel safe and secure and begin to understand and believe that we are Mummy and Daddy and they would be with us for ever more.

How We Began To Build Our Girls' Trust And Security

We obviously showered the girls with love and kindness and provided them with everything they needed the second they needed it. To some people it may have appeared like we were spoiling the girls, but we knew that it was necessary to help them to understand that we were reliable and trustworthy people. We needed to do this as, in the past, when their needs hadn't been met, they had learnt that adults were not people that they could always trust.

This is something that we had to teach them and by constantly meeting their needs instantly and becoming attuned to them, like a parent should in the first few hours after birth, we could help them to understand that they could always trust us to look after them properly and nurture them.

We had to rebuild and put back the missing pieces that they had not had in their lives. It was explained to us like a wall and if the pieces near to the foundations were not stable or had bricks missing, then the wall would fall down and crumble. If a child has missed out on their basic needs being met as babies it is vital that you rebuild this stage of their development, even if this means giving them toys, equipment or activities that are meant for children of a younger age or developmental stage. Otherwise they will find it very hard to move on or develop effectively in later life.

For us this meant treating our 2 year old like a baby again, giving her bottles of milk, a dummy and a special soft toy, rocking her and holding her like a baby and singing lullabies to her. In addition, we did play activities that were aimed at babies, then gradually moving on to the next stage when we felt that she had gained everything that she had needed from these activities and was ready to move on.

We recognised that our eldest didn't know how to play, so we spent time teaching her how to play with toys and did lots of role play which she loved.

Our baby was only 9 months old, so was obviously still at the baby stage, but we ensured that we constantly and effectively met her needs so she could relax and trust us. We ensured that we went over all the previous baby stages with her too so we could be confident that she had not missed out on anything to help her as she grows and develops.

We dedicated our lives to spending every minute of the day with our girls so either myself or my husband were constantly with them to help them to gain trust that we would always be there and they wouldn't just be left with anybody as unfortunately had happened to them before we became Mummy and Daddy. This would give them the security to relax and trust us each day, knowing that wherever they went

Mummy and Daddy were always there with them to aid bonding and attachment and to help them to become safe and secure little girls, who would thrive

We discussed with the extended family and friends that over the first few months when they visited they needed to always direct the girls back to us for their needs to be met. We kindly asked everyone to say to the girls "Mummy and Daddy will do that for you," or "Go and ask Mummy and Daddy for that" if the girls asked visitors for things or to do things for them. By doing this it was teaching the girls that Mummy and Daddy were always the people that would meet their needs.

Unlike most children who learn from birth that their parents are their main caregivers, and will do everything for them, our girls had never had this necessity in their lives. They needed to learn, that this is Mummy and Daddy's role, and that we are the people to trust to meet their every need.

We constantly told the girls that we loved them and brought 'family' (Mummy, Daddy and our babies' names) into all aspects of life and play so they could begin to understand who their family was. We gave them lots of opportunity to talk about family and explained what this meant and that we would always be together now as a family.

It was essential for them to feel secure and trust that nobody would ever come into our house and pick them up and take them off. In their past this had been a very frequent occurrence and they had no say in whether or not this happened.

They had no voice and no way of saying "NO" to certain situations when social workers, support workers, respite foster carers etc would collect them and take them off to unfamiliar houses or social services buildings. It still fills me with sadness to imagine how frightening this must have been to two such young children who had no understanding of what was happening or why and feeling totally helpless and scared with strangers. As adults we know who these people are, but a child doesn't understand this.

We observed that when anybody came to visit us, our eldest especially, would either cling to myself or her Daddy or hide in a corner and get upset and it became clear that she was worried about being taken away from us.

On our baby's first birthday, which was three months after the girls came to live with us, we had a tea party to celebrate and invited grandparents, aunties, uncles and cousins. At the time this seemed a normal thing to do but looking back, we shouldn't have done this, as it really unsettled the girls.

Having all of these visitors around must have triggered past memories and insecurities. When people got up to leave at the end of the tea party and were saying goodbye to us, our eldest became hysterical and said, "But I don't want to go, I want to be with you Mummy and Daddy". She obviously thought that she was going to have to say goodbye to us and leave as these other people were going and she became very upset and insecure. It was heartbreaking to think that, in her little mind, she thought that she had to leave us, but it did show that she had bonded and attached to us, which was very positive.

This highlighted to us how things can appear through our girls' eyes, and whilst WE understand that the girls are ours forever, it was going to take a lot of time and constant reassurance for them to trust and believe that we are a forever family now and they will never be separated from us.

We decided to stop having visitors altogether for a fortnight and cocoon the girls in our little family, without seeing anybody else or have anybody round to visit, so we could begin to build their trust and help them to feel safe and secure following the party.

We didn't visit anybody else's house for at least a month, although we did go out as a family to parks and attractions and in general everyday life situations. We just didn't have close contact with other adults so the girls didn't feel insecure about adults coming and taking them away from their home or Mummy and Daddy. We also did lots of work with our eldest to help her to understand that she was in control of herself and other people wouldn't come and pick her up, kiss her or take her away from us, to give her a feeling of being in control.

When we did begin to have visitors again, we asked them to be very calm and come in and speak to us (adults) and only interact with the girls on the girls' terms when the girls wanted them to. We also asked everyone else not to go into the girls' personal space so they didn't feel threatened in any way and didn't have to worry about being picked up by strangers.

We asked everyone else not to kiss the girls, pick them up, sit them on their knees, etc. as this was invading the girls' personal space and causing our eldest especially to feel insecure. Obviously we, as Mummy and Daddy, gave the girls lots of love, hugs and cuddles as we all needed this. They were happy and comfortable with this and enjoyed our affection.

By doing this, our eldest soon learnt that she was in control of situations even when other adults were in the same room and she began to trust that nobody would come into our house and pick her up or take her off. If she said "No" to anything, everyone would respect it, giving her an understanding that she has her own voice that would be listened to, has her own independence and a sense of self control.

We also had an amazing Health Visitor who was very knowledgeable and she suggested for us to do massage techniques, massaging her hands, arms and legs and telling her this is hers and nobody else's, to give her power over herself.

We were amazed at how well all of these strategies worked and very quickly the girls became much more relaxed when we had visitors and within a few months she no longer became distressed, or hid in corners when we had visitors.

I know it was very hard for the grandparents, especially, not to be 'hands on' with the girls but these strategies were really working and benefitting our girls. It was lovely to see the girls being so much more relaxed around visitors and the grandparents were very supportive.

Nobody else looked after the girls for two years and they were always with either me or my husband as we knew this was important for them, to help them to trust and understand that they could rely on Mummy and Daddy to meet their every need and help them to feel safe and secure.

The girls are now very secure and have a better understanding that we are a forever family and that they will never be separated from us. These strategies worked brilliantly and really helped the girls to bond and attach securely with us.

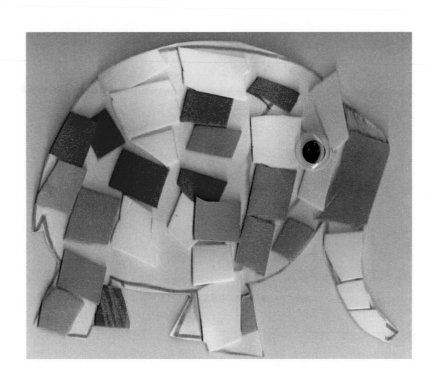

121

Social Workers' Visits Once We Became Mummy & Daddy

For the first month after the girls came home forever we continued to have contact with our Adoption Social Worker or the girls' social worker on a weekly basis, as is protocol for all children that are adopted. The social workers would visit on alternate weeks so we only had one per week visiting.

Obviously they needed to ensure that the girls were happy and settling well, they would offer any advice should we have needed it and were very supportive. We were lucky and everything was going brilliantly with the girls but it was nice to see the social workers for a coffee and a chat and was also reassuring for them to see how well the girls were settling with us and how happy they were.

The social workers were like close friends now, we had seen so much of each other and know each other so well. They were instrumental in uniting us with our babies for which we would be eternally grateful, so we were glad to see them and to share with them how well we were all settling as a family together.

It was also nice for the girls' social worker, who had worked with our girls from the beginning when they were in the birth family and seen what a poor start they had in life, seeing them happy with their forever family now having a loving and fulfilling life.

After the first month we all had a review meeting at our house, which was attended by our social workers and the Social Services Manager, to discuss how everything was going. As everything was perfect, it was decided that we only needed to have monthly visits from the social workers from now onward. These would continue until we would go to court to get the Adoption Order and be classed as a 'normal family'. We could apply for the Adoption Order once the girls had lived with us for at least ten weeks.

Adoption Order Application

The Adoption Order is an order made by the court that makes you the legal parent of the child or children that you are adopting and gives you all of the normal parental rights and responsibilities for your child.

Before you can apply for the Adoption Order, the children need to have lived with you for at least 10 weeks. Once both you and the social workers are all in agreement that you are ready to apply for the Adoption Order, the social worker completes all of the relevant paperwork to apply to court for the Adoption Order. Then, once all of the paperwork has been submitted to the courts, you have to wait for the court to send you a date when the Adoption Order Hearing will take place.

In our case we applied to the courts for an Adoption Hearing when the girls had lived with us for 10 weeks in the December and, after a few weeks, we received a letter from the Court to inform us that our Adoption Hearing was scheduled for a date in the following March. Obviously adoption is a legal process so that is the reason why the courts are involved and the Judge has the ultimate decision on whether the Adoption Order is made.

126

The Morning Of Our Adoption Hearing

The morning had arrived when we knew that our Adoption Order would hopefully be made; the final nerve wracking day in the Adoption Process before our Forever Family became official and we were legally our babies' parents. We would have complete parental responsibility, as much as if the girls were birth children and they would be given our surname.

Such a special and important day! We couldn't help feeling very anxious but hoped and prayed that everything would be successful and the Judge would grant the Adoption Order.

Unfortunately, both our social worker and the girls' social worker were on annual leave so neither of them could attend the court hearing. We were informed that a member of the social services staff was going to attend and then call us as soon as the order had been made.

We were allowed to attend, but were advised not to by the courts as sometimes birth parents may attend this final hearing and that could have been awkward and breach our confidentiality.

We therefore waited anxiously all morning and hadn't heard anything by lunchtime so we decided to call the social services office. To our disappointment, nobody was available who knew anything about our case and I was informed that the person who was actually meant to be in court and ringing us following our Adoption Hearing was actually also on annual leave!

Our most important official day and I couldn't speak to anyone to see if the order had been granted! So, unable to wait any longer, I decided to phone the courts directly and, to our relief and joy, I was informed by a very friendly employee at the courts that 'YES' we were now legally Mummy and Daddy to our gorgeous baby girls.

Massive hugs and endless tears of joy, the reasons for which our babies were too young to properly understand. We were now officially a Happy Forever Family: what an amazing and unforgettable day, a date that we would remember forever.

Our Celebration Day

We were invited to court the week after the Adoption Order was granted for our Celebration Day. This is when you attend the court with your children, family, friends and social workers to celebrate the Adoption Order being granted and officially becoming a Forever Family.

We dressed the girls in their pretty new dresses that we had bought for this very special day and they looked like beautiful little princesses. We invited the grandparents to come to the Celebration Day along with our adoption social worker and the girls' social worker.

We were mindful not to invite too many people as this was going to be quite an overwhelming day for our girls, in a strange courtroom with a judge and court staff, who were all strangers to them. As they were so young, they couldn't really understand why we were going to this strange courtroom, so we kept it as low key as possible so not to unsettle them.

It was a lovely morning and the judge that granted our Adoption Order chatted with us all, a large chest of toys was provided in the court room for our girls to play with whilst the judge had an informal chat with us. The judge then gave them a special certificate and let them try on his wig but they declined! He gave us the Official Adoption Order Paperwork and explained to us that the court would send the necessary paperwork off and we would receive the girls' new Adoption Certificates with their new names on, which you use the same as Birth Certificates.

The judge then took us through to the courtroom where the Adoption Order was granted so that we could take pictures and have our pictures taken with the Judge.

Our social worker also gave our girls a little present which was a lovely gesture.

Our Celebration Day was held at 10am and lasted about an hour so we decided to all go for breakfast afterwards in a nearby café which the girls loved, eating their favourite food-sausages- to celebrate!

131

Saying Goodbye To Our Social Workers

Now we are officially a Forever Family and our Adoption Order has been granted we no longer need our social workers, as we are classed as a 'Normal Family'. It was therefore time to say goodbye to them which was quite emotional.

Our social worker had grown to know us inside out and knew every finest detail about us from our initial visit when we first met her, through our amazing Adoption Journey where she was with us every step of the way. She was the person who first told us all about our babies and had been there through introductions until now when we are officially Mummy and Daddy to our girls.

We therefore have got to know her so well and have immense respect for her. We will be forever grateful to her for the work she did to enable us to adopt our angels.

How can you thank somebody for helping you to receive the best gift in life, two amazingly beautiful daughters? We decided to get her a really nice card, writing a very personal thank you message inside, and bought her a chocolate teddy with a thank you message iced onto it. We thought that she would be embarrassed by a big gift but could tell that she was touched with what we had given to her and she knew how thankful we were.

We also did the same for the girls' social worker who had played a huge part in helping to safeguard our babies before we had the honour of becoming their Mummy and Daddy; taking them into care when her endless work with the birth family wasn't improving their situation, through to playing her part in finding us as their Mummy and Daddy and being there every step of our adoption journey once we had been matched with our girls.

It was strange at first without regular visits from the social workers but we have kept in touch regularly by email and our social worker occasionally pops in for a chat if she is in the area which is lovely.

134

Life As Our Little Family

Our life is now perfect! The girls have lived with us for nearly three years now and are growing up far too fast. They amaze us every single day and the love that we share is incredible.

Yes, we do have our little hurdles which we have to overcome, as children who have been adopted usually have additional needs, caused by their previous neglect or abuse and not having their needs appropriately met whilst they were young. This will need to be worked on, to put all of the little building blocks securely into place to enable them to progress with their emotional and intellectual development.

Many children being adopted have also unfortunately been exposed to alcohol while in the womb which can cause them to have Foetal Alcohol Syndrome. This is a life - long condition that cannot be cured, but parents need to research and educate themselves on, so they can best support their children. They will need to help them cope with life and everyday situations, which can be very difficult and overwhelming for children with Foetal Alcohol Syndrome and this requires a special type of parenting.

Our girls are a total inspiration and we have so much fun, love and laughter together, every day is one of joy and happiness. We are now a normal happy family and enjoy everything that life offers. We have already shared so many special moments and fantastic experiences with our beautiful princesses and love them so dearly.

Life Story Work

Life story work is vitally important for all children who have been adopted to gain a sense of themselves, their lives so far and their identity.

It helps them to understand what has happened and why during their lives, and although it may seem daunting to begin with for fear of upsetting or unsettling your children, it soon becomes apparent, just how important this is.

I was very conscious that I wanted to begin this with our girls from a very young age but had to consider the best way to do this with a nine month and a two year old. We wanted to do this successfully and felt apprehensive about doing or saying something wrong or something that could be misinterpreted by a very young child.

The way we approached this was to make a photo album of their lives so far, very simply with a photo of the birth parents, then a few photos with the foster carers until when they came to live with us. Then we did photos of us together, trying to keep this is date order to show the sequence of events, like their first outing with Mummy and Daddy, their first car journey in our car etc. Then they could build a visual memory of their lives and their life events in the order that they occurred to begin to gain an understanding of their life history.

Our girls love looking at photographs and naturally ask questions, so we were able to look through their photos with them and identify who everyone was and explain their lives to them through the pictures, which has worked very successfully.

Even at their young age, it really helped them to gain an understanding of their lives before we became a Forever Family and the photographs have successfully enabled them to build a visual picture in their minds of who everybody was and what they looked like. We feel that this is important for them to be able to do this so they do not develop an inaccurate or misconceived view of what their birth parents or foster carers looked like.

We also believe in being very honest with the girls about why they needed a Forever Family and that their birth parents were not able to look after or care for them properly in a way that they deserved. We are very careful that we do this in an age and developmentally appropriate manner so they don't become distressed or overwhelmed, but we do give them the basic reasons, that we can extend on in the future when they are developmentally and emotionally at an age to learn more about their lives.

For now though, they are both happy, relaxed and content about their little life story and becoming a Forever Family. They occasionally ask questions about their lives before we became their Mummy and Daddy but it's usually about things like what shopping trolley seat they would have sat in when they were babies- the lie back or sitting up type- or what food they used to eat or the toys they played with, rather than any intense questions.

We have found that the more you talk about and discuss their life story, the easier it becomes. I remember when we first began this with the girls, I always felt very emotional and have vivid memories of welling up with tears in the early days when we first began the life story work. I felt so upset and emotional about how people in their early lives had let them down so badly, not looking after our two amazingly beautiful and precious, innocent babies, who deserved to have been given the best possible start in life that they were so cruelly denied.

Our girls also love to hear all about when Mummy and Daddy were waiting for them to come and live with us forever and what we did to get ready for them, preparing their bedrooms and decorating them, buying their new toys, clothes, cots and pushchairs and everything they could possibly need. This is also a lovely way for us to explain to them how excited we were, how we got everything they liked ready for them and how we were always thinking about them, even before they came to live with us.

Although I will always feel sad about what our girls suffered when babies, discussing their life journey does become easier and it reminds us of how lucky we all are now to be together in our loving Forever Family. Our babies will now always have the best possible childhood and have all the love and care in the world from their doting Mummy and Daddy.

Advice For Anybody Who Is Thinking Of Adopting.

If anybody reading this is thinking of embarking on their own Adoption Journey to become a Forever Family, I can honestly say that adoption has been the best thing that my husband and I have ever done in our lives. Adopting has enabled us to have the beautiful family that we so desperately wanted and, now we have our daughters, our lives are complete.

For us, the love we have for our daughters is so great, we couldn't possibly love them any more. If they were birth children, the love that we have for them would be no different, as we love them with all our hearts.

We are just a normal family now and, looking at us, we are no different to people who have given birth to their children. We love our girls unconditionally and every day is one shared with love and happiness. We often get people who don't know us passing comment in a shop or at a toddler group saying, "Oh doesn't your little girl look like you", or "She is her Daddy's double" and yes I have to smile and agree. You definitely grow as a family, we agree that the girls have grown to look like us and take on our mannerisms and characteristics, to a point that nobody would ever know that our girls are adopted unless they know us.

I would urge anybody thinking of adopting to contact their Local Authority Adoption Department or an Adoption Agency to find out more information to see if adoption is right for them. In our experience the Adoption Social Workers couldn't have been more friendly or approachable and they really put us at ease throughout our Adoption Journey, right from the initial phone call that we made to them.

Adopting our beautiful daughters and becoming a Forever Family really has been a magical and very happy experience for us. I hope other people who are considering adoption are able to embark on their own Adoption Journeys and experience immense happiness and pleasure in their own Forever Families as we have in ours.

Thank You To Our Amazing Babies

To our gorgeous angels, the main reason for Mummy wanting to write this book is for you two. I wanted to record and explain every step of our Adoption Journey because, at the moment, you are both too young to understand all of this. When you are old enough, which you will be when you are reading this book, I believed it was important that you should be able to read this book about the amazing Adoption Journey we shared, so that we could become your Mummy and Daddy and you to be our precious little daughters.

We love you both so dearly; you make us happy and proud every second of each day and we are so lucky and honoured to be your Mummy and Daddy.

You are so precious to us, darlings, and you both are immensely special and amazingly gorgeous girls. The day that we became your Mummy and Daddy was the happiest day of our lives.

Mummy and Daddy had waited all of our lives for you and we will love, cherish, protect and adore you Forever and Ever. XXXX

Ps. Thank you both for the amazing artwork you both created to illustrate our book. XXXX